Poems

Changes

Valerie Cafariella

BookLeaf Publishing

India | USA | UK

Made with ❤ on the BookLeaf Publishing Platform
www.bookleafpub.in
www.bookleafpub.com

Dedication

I would like to dedicate this poetry book to my family. To my husband Wayne, who has always believed in me. To my four children, Wayne, Jordan, Christie Lynn, and Lindsay Marie. Alot of what I write and feel comes from raising and spending time with you. To my two beautiful grandchildren Coral Mae, and Mason Anthony, you are growing up so fast!!! I hope you save this book always as the memory of us!

Preface

This book of poems started with me waking up between three and four in the morning with the words of these poems in my head. I was compelled to write them down. I was taken back by this experience, even though I had always wanted to write poetry since about the age of seven when I first read Robert Louis Stevenson's poems, "A Child's Garden of Verses."

I have committed this year to writing. Since January, I have written over 30 poems. Some are good and some need work.

I also want to lean into the topic of my transition from motherhood to empty nest, to aging of myself. another dynamic, the grief process: caring for my mom after the loss of my dad. She has been very strong during this time, though it has been difficult for me to watch. I have experienced many strong emotions that this life had not prepared me for during this transitional time.

About motherhood, you identify as a mom raising children, that is your identity for a season, and you are consumed with their care and upbringing as well as their emotional health. But one day the door shuts and they are gone. They found their wings so to say and have flown from your nest. You are left with the pieces of a life that was so busy and noisy to a quiet house and yourself. This new beginning is a very painful one and needs a lot of prayer and support through it, but the support may not come from the ones you have cared for, for so long. You will embark on finding your people, the people that will be there for you as you create the new you.

Acknowledgements

I would like to thank my parents for providing for me a wonderful childhood and experiences that molded and made me into who I am today. I want to thank my siblings, my sister for being my closest lifelong friend, who we share a love for beautiful things and Christmas. For my brother who is always positive and someone I can always talk to, and for his incredible gift of music and guitar playing. I am glad I introduced you to the iconic rock bands of the 1970's!!

1. The Transition

Slumber evades me, I lie here in the gray muteness, it is
the middle of the night. I am alone with vague misty
memories of my young children's chatter reeling through
my mind.
I hear the faint sound of a dog barking in the distance
which reminds me of my daughter's golden dog, who is
now gone.
That was a past life; as if I were an actress in a scenario,
a mother to four children.
The emotions in the skit were strong and mournful
tearing at the core of my being.
All of the bittersweet years have found their wings and
have flown away.
The show is over, the curtain goes down, I walk off the
stage.
I am awake now, I am alone, waiting for a new role to
perform.
What shall it be? Who shall I become?
Quietness and time have become a friend to me.
This has replaced the years of noisy chaos; this is so

foreign to me.
The sun starts to rise in the east as it always does,
shining on new possibilities.

2. Mornings

A blanket covers me as I sit in my morning chair.
The sunlight beaming in spreading its golden warmth.
I contemplate my day.
What will I do? Where will I start? Will I write about
nature, or a white sandy beach?
Or will I write about the condition of my heart?
The words come to me like a faithful friend, reassuring
me. I write down my thoughts that develop into prose.
I choose the beach, it makes my heart feel light. It is the
place I like to go to, to make everything right. It is here
where I let go of my worries, fears, and concerns into the
waters at the shore.
I walk along the sand collecting shells which become my
treasures to take back with me so when I look at them, I
will have the memory of the sea. I forget my cares for an
hour or so.
I sit and watch the swelling waves; they are mesmerizing
to me. If you don't know where I am, I may be by the sea,
where the sand now covers me.

3. Cresent Moon

I sit on top of a crescent moon between heaven and earth
I bask in the glow of its wonderful light looking at things
below
I notice that I am happy, without a care in the world
I feel magical almost in a trance, as I lean back and give
the stars a glance
Something catches my eye; I think it is a shooting star
going by, when I start to wobble.
I start falling slowly down to earth, I see the stars
shining bright, when all of a sudden
I wake up, to only realize that I was dreaming

4. Sleepless

I am up again during the early watches of dawn.
When creatures scatter about looking for morsels to
store in their dens.
The sky appears as velvety darkness with hints of first
light. The clouds are waiting to be illuminated with
colors.
Purple, orange, and yellow as the sun rises and the birds
start to sing, some are loud, some are faint, all a chorus
of new beginnings.
Day has dawned, the sun reaching up from the eastern
sky, it is faithful and can be trusted again.
A new day of possibility to use my time wisely, to
contemplate, to pray. To wait on internal instruction,
that is given to me, bit by bit as a spoon fed child.
I am ready now to go about my day filled with hope and
desire to breathe, to live and love again.

5. Waking

Where does the first impulse or thought come from upon
waking in the early morning dawn?
Does it come from the deep recesses of my mind where
dreams intermingle with reality.
Why is it that some of my thoughts seem so foreign that
I have to harness them so I can be calm and experience
peace. Are they the circumstances, challenges and
situations that have occurred in my past, that only come
to haunt me?
But now I am in the present, and the past is my history
that I don't have to live again.
I find myself becoming clearer as I wake up. It is me
myself and my thoughts.
I am determined to make my life work. I rouse myself to
make some coffee. This will help me connect into my
day.

6. The Flame

Candles shining brightly in the darkness of the night,
keeping me awake to its glow so bright.
The flame dances around by the nights draft, only to
simmer down to a steady stream of light.
I write at my desk words that fill the page of daytimes
that led to a lifetime that has past.
So I hope that my life continues to flicker on some more,
until the day the candle light blows out and I am no
more.

7. Essence

Can your skin hold all your essence in?
You breathe in and out as you feel the suns warmth
penetrate deep within you.
As if time stands still.
Your soul wrestles to receive what it needs to just be;
needing nothing at the moment.
Here I am laying in the sand on the beach serene, the
cares of this world seem to fade with each incoming
wave.
Body, mind, and soul are one.
Recharge
A much needed rest from the monotony of everyday life.
Will my footprints in the sand melt away all of the chaos
of my mind?
My skin feels hot then it clashes with the cool water and
its salty spray.
Your essence has been renewed for another day.

8. Moonlight

Moonlight so bright, changes the night time sky.
What normally can be dark is now illuminated and
magical putting on its show.
Monochromatic shadows appear on the earth below.
The glow penetrates through the trees, forests, plains,
beaches, and deserts its effect is not all the same.
It seems like the moonlight makes time stand still, where
lovers rest in the light as it casts its spell.

9. Our tears tell a story

The wet tear dripped down my cheek as I feel the grief
that has captured my soul.
Why, I say, why?
These tears keep coming and won't stop, I can't control
them, they control me as if I am being kidnapped or
taken hostage. I am now under their spell and only time
will tell the type of person I will now be.
I don't remember the person I was before anymore. I am
changed. My history is now written in the eulogy of the
life you lived.
Life has taken a new plot twist, life without you, how
will I exist? Now I find myself picking up the puzzle
pieces of me off the floor to have lost the most important
piece, now that you are gone.
The first morning, the first day, they are not joyful
anymore. Your shirt, your comb are here, they have
always been here, though I see them very differently
now. Should I put them away, hide them, they are traces
of you, but I can't find you or hear your voice, you are
gone.

I cry again this time deeply as if all my lifetime fears
have come to visit me. I am haunted. How do I do this?
THIS! what do I call this? Existence? Pain? Grief has
visited me and it is here to stay. I am no longer the same.
My smile is different as well as my laugh, they have been
washed out by the tears and pain. I keep breathing and
bleeding inside hoping, praying for these feelings to
subside, but they don't. I go over to the mirror and see
my eyes full of pain, swollen and red from griefs rain.

10. The Hurricane

The wind was whirling at half past three, I got out of bed
to look at the trees.
They were bending and swaying for what I could see,
was this the predicted storm of the century?
I created a mental list, "Do I have milk, eggs, butter, and
flour? My grandmother always said, " If you have all
these ingredients, you can always bake a cake!"
All these thoughts swirling around my head would I
have enough time to prepare?
I hear in the distance an owl hoot as if it was an omen or
some kind of fate. I was hoping I was ready and not to
late.
It was time to hunker down, the weatherman said the
storm was named "*Ian,*" *a category five.* So if you weren't
ready then it is time to pray.
Where were my candles and matches? I made some
coffee, it started to brew. The whiff of it went through
the house as I was settling in. I found an old book, but I
couldn't read, I plopped it down, my anxiety heightened
as I looked again at the trees, they were bending and

swaying now violently.

The eye of the storm was now over head, it would deceive us into thinking things would calm down. Then the rain pelted down in a ferocious way. The air turned a hue of green, it was the eeriest thing that I have ever seen.

The lights started to flicker about to go out, when I heard a loud crash outside that made me jump! A large tree went down to the ground, it laid there uprooted a strange sight to see.

All I could do was wait as the wind continued to howl, it sounded like a witch who was out on a prowl.

I must have dosed off to wake up to the sun shining a very welcome friend after a stormy night.

I ventured out the front door to survey any damage, I looked down my street and saw down trees and debris. It seemed the storm subsided and the power was restored. I survived another hurricane , I can't tell anymore.

11. Words

My written words heal me and give me a place to go.
A place that is secret for only me to know.
I will share my words in time when I feel safe, but for
right now they will stay in my safe place close to my
soul.

12. The Problem

I am not sure who I am anymore, it is not easy for me,
even if I try.
The person I have changed into has white hair, I look
into the mirror and the younger me is no longer there.
The wrinkles that surround my baby blue eyes have
changed my looks, I have been smitten.
The problem is that I am old, not in my heart though.
Life has crept up on me and doesn't seem right, they say
embrace yourself, well I will try, but I do miss the
younger me.

13. Me

I am, I will be patient with thee.

From the rising sun, to the sunset by the sea.

These years have changed me.

I use to be ten steps ahead, rushing into everything not

really present just me.

But I've learned that in this life we need to sometimes be

still, to think, to dream, to love, to be free.

Free from all the chatter, opinions and angst like a little

child just trusting filled with wonder to climb up a tree.

So I will leave you with these thoughts that came from

deep within me to share with you the true one and only

me.

14. Rain

Silver raindrops drip down the window pane catching
the sunlight in its small frame.
The rain has stopped and we can go outside again.
The grass is wet and green, the earth is brand new, each
leaf and flower has a sparkling drop of dew.
A rainbow appears up in the luminous sky, the colors so
vibrant putting on their display making sure the storm
clouds are barreling away.
The birds are singing and flying above as if to say, "this is
the weather we love!"

15. Peace like a veil

Your peace is like a veil that falls gently over me, as I sit
here in the dark.
I need this time of silence and surrender away from all
distractions, noise and quest.
To manage becoming who I am meant to be.
Why has it taken so many years of lost dreams, fears and
solemn tears?
I look back and think of what I could have created, but I
always seemed stuck; caught between what I wanted to
do, verses what I had to do.
But this life is not through with me yet! I don't have time
to waste! I must become what I was meant to be and live
for my purpose.
So I will succumb to writing my words to release them
from my heart to this world, and if this world doesn't
receive them, then I really don't care because they are
not stuck inside my heart.

16. Swimming

What would it be like to swim effortlessly into a crystal
blue sea?
I would start off slow to enjoy the feeling and know that
being in the water would send my soul reeling.
I would raise my arms and my legs would flutter and as
I moved along, my brain would unclutter.
I would taste the saltiness of the sea and know that soon
this would become a memory.
So in these moments of sweet peace, I will linger here
floating around.

17. Tired

Where is the drive that was once in me?
Like it use to be?
I'd wake up and start my day running so to say.
My energy has changed it took time, the years have
accumulated.
It is a strange feeling.
You hang onto anything in you to feel young again.
Bones creak, muscles ache, wrinkles appear like cruel
fate.
You feel trapped not knowing how to get out of this
cocoon or shroud over you.
Though a butterfly won't emerge, instead its now an
older version of you.

18. To be still

I want to be still with you
to feel your peace through and through
To rest in your presence to be made new
Yesterday is gone, I don't have to feel that way anymore,
defeated, hopeless, lost.
I will embrace this new day and receive it as a gift to
cherish to unfold it to embrace it.
I find this gift is what I needed more time to spent with
you.
Thank you for loving me with all my fears and doubts.
So I will look into the mirror and see myself as you see
me, whole, forgiven, a loved child.

19. Love

Wonderment and glory they fill my head thinking of the
words you lovingly said.
This is that you love me heart, soul, and mind for I will
be your lover for this lifetime.
What we will share together the triumphs of this life,
with your hand in my hand no matter what the strife
We will weather the joys and sorrows together this much
is true, for I will always be, my love, devoted to you

20. The memory of you

The memory of you is like a song that plays on in my
head.
When I wake up in the morning and when I go to bed.
It is haunting and faint, but the song plays on and on.
The lyrics are sweet of a time when we were happy, but
all that is over and gone.
When we kiss by the river for the very first time, and I
felt your heartbeat next to mine.
We were lost in that moment that was frozen in time,
you pledged your love to me and said that you would
always be mine.
The days turned to weeks to become a year, but word
was sent to me that you were no longer here.
You left on a Sunday as the sun was setting, I was beside
myself it was so upsetting.
How could you leave me hanging like that? With no way
to reach you so you could explain.
It all turns out I was never yours in your heart as you
were in mine. You took what you wanted from me and
didn't care about how this would play out.

So, the tune lingers and plays in my head, the memory of
you is if you are dead.
My heart is broken, I am left with all the pieces that will
take me a lifetime to get over you.

21. My heart is in your hands

My heart is in your hands on this new day as we start
our life together.
We will ride the storms as the come, with your hand in
my hand we will make it through.
So, on this special day when our love is brand new, I will
make a vow to you, to always be true.
I look into the eyes of this handsome young man,
knowing that someday you will be an older man.
When that day comes, I will still love you cause my
hearts in your hands, and I'll always be true.

www.ingramcontent.com/pod-product-compliance
Lightning Source LLC
Chambersburg PA
CBHW071240140726
47996CB00007B/2685